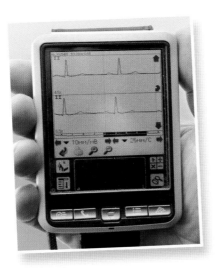

Published in 2013 by The Rosen Publishing Group, Inc.
29 East 21st Street, New York, NY 10010

Photo Credits: **KEY** tl=top left; tc=top center; tr=top right; cl=center left; c=center; cr=center right; bl=bottom left; bc=bottom center; br=bottom right

CBT = Corbis; DSCD = Digital Stock; DT = Dreamstime; GI = Getty Images; iS = istockphoto.com; N = NASA; SH = Shutterstock; TF = Topfoto; TPL = photolibrary.com

front cover c SH; bg, br TPL; **back cover** tl SH; bc TPL; **1**c CBT; **2–3**tc iS; **4–5**cl CBT; **6**tc SH; **7**tr iS; bc SH; cl, tl TPL; **8**cl DT; bl TPL; **8–9**bc TPL; tc SH; **9**tr iS; br TPL; **10**bl iS; cr TPL; **11**br, tc SH; **12**bl SH; **12–13**bc iS; tr TPL; **13**br TPL; **14–15**bc GI; tl TPL; **15**br TF; tr TPL; **16**bc TPL; **16–17**tc TPL; **17**bl TF; **18**c SH; **19**bl TF; **20**br SH; bl, tr TPL; **21**c courtesy of Magnetic Source Imaging Center of Minnesota Epilepsy Group, P.A. and United Hospital at Saint Paul, Minnesota, USA; bl courtesy of Michael Weisend, Mind Research Network, New Mexico, USA; **22**bc, cl CBT; br, cr iS; tr SH; **24**cr CBT; cl GI; c TF; **24–25**tc CBT; **25**bl, tr CBT; br GI; **26**cr iS; bl TF; **27**cr SH; br TPL; **28**bc iS; tr N; **29**tl, tr CBT; bc TPL; **30**br iS; c, cr, tr TF

All illustrations copyright Weldon Owen Pty Ltd.

Weldon Owen Pty Ltd
Managing Director: Kay Scarlett
Creative Director: Sue Burk
Publisher: Helen Bateman
Senior Vice President, International Sales: Stuart Laurence
Vice President Sales North America: Ellen Towell
Administration Manager, International Sales: Kristine Ravn

Library of Congress Cataloging-in-Publication Data

McFadzean, Lesley.
Technology and treatments / by Lesley McFadzean. — 1st ed.
     p. cm. — (Discovery education: technology)
Includes index.
ISBN 978-1-4488-7886-4 (library binding) — ISBN 978-1-4488-7968-7 (pbk.) —
ISBN 978-1-4488-7974-8 (6-pack)
1. Medical technology—Juvenile literature. 2. Medical innovations—Juvenile literature. I. Title.
R855.4.M34 2012
610.1'4—dc23

2011051556

Manufactured in the United States of America

CPSIA Compliance Information: Batch #SW12PK: For Further Information contact Rosen Publishing, New York, New York at 1-800-237-9932

TECHNOLOGY AND TREATMENTS

LESLEY MCFADZEAN

PowerKiDS
press™

New York

Contents

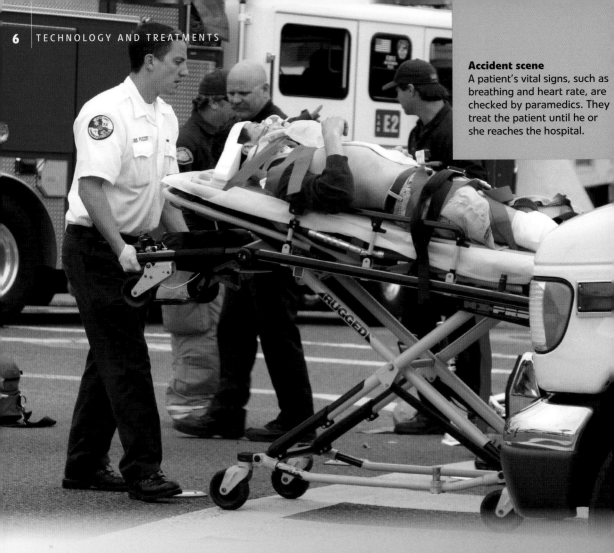

Accident scene
A patient's vital signs, such as breathing and heart rate, are checked by paramedics. They treat the patient until he or she reaches the hospital.

Accident and Emergency

When an ambulance rushes to an accident, it has medical technology onboard. The people who use this are called paramedics. They give portable oxygen to a patient with breathing problems. They can try to restart a heart with a defibrillator, a machine that delivers electric shocks through the patient's chest. When the patient is ready for transportation, special stretchers, boards, and collars make sure the patient's injuries are not made any worse.

Did You Know?
Ambulances were first used in the Crusades of the eleventh century. The Knights of St. John brought the wounded in horse-drawn carriages from the battlefield to hospital tents.

Cervical collar
A cervical collar, or neck brace, is put around a patient's neck before moving him to reduce the risk of paralysis.

Portable oxygen
Paramedics carry oxygen masks and tanks to give oxygen to both children and adults, if necessary.

Special stretcher
Sometimes an ambulance cannot reach an accident scene, so paramedics must practice moving stretchers across difficult ground.

Backboard
Before moving a person with an injured, possibly broken, back, paramedics immobilize the person's body on a backboard.

Checking on the Patient

I n the past, the only way to check on a patient was at their bedside. A nurse or doctor took a patient's temperature, checked blood pressure, and listened to the heart with a stethoscope. In hospitals today, it is possible to check on a patient's vital signs without being near them. Wired up to new technology, the patient's body is automatically monitored.

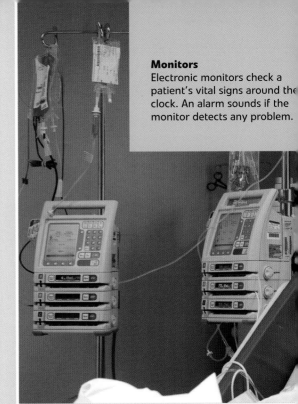

Monitors
Electronic monitors check a patient's vital signs around the clock. An alarm sounds if the monitor detects any problem.

Diabetes
This microchip tester measures blood sugar levels in a spot of blood from a patient who has diabetes.

Spirometer
The lung function of an asthmatic is measured when she breathes out hard into a spirometer.

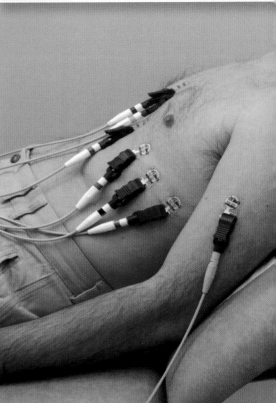

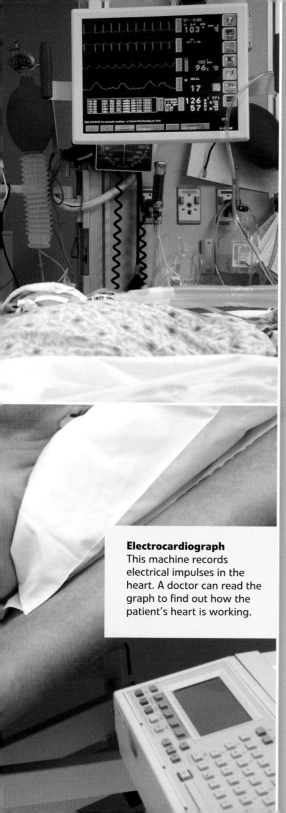

Stethoscopes

A doctor uses a stethoscope to amplify, or increase, sounds from a patient's heart or lungs. The sound from ordinary stethoscopes can be overwhelmed by background noise, but ultrasound stethoscopes work in noisy environments.

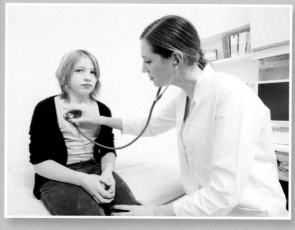

Regular stethoscope
A regular stethoscope picks up normal, audible sounds when it is used to listen to the heart or lungs.

Electrocardiograph
This machine records electrical impulses in the heart. A doctor can read the graph to find out how the patient's heart is working.

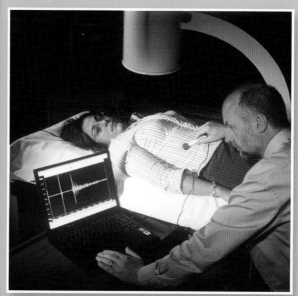

Ultrasound stethoscope
This sends high-frequency, ultrasound waves into the body. Internal organs bounce the sound waves back to a monitor.

Looking Inside

Until the late nineteenth century, doctors could only guess what might be happening inside a patient's body. A bone might be broken, but the doctor could not be certain. In 1896, German scientist Wilhelm Röntgen discovered what he called X-rays. These invisible rays pass through skin and muscle to reveal the bones beneath. X-rays are still used widely today, alongside newer technologies, such as magnetic resonance imaging (MRI) and ultrasound, to provide images of internal organs.

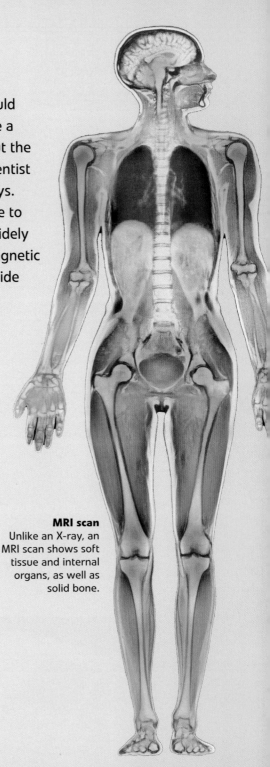

MRI scan
Unlike an X-ray, an MRI scan shows soft tissue and internal organs, as well as solid bone.

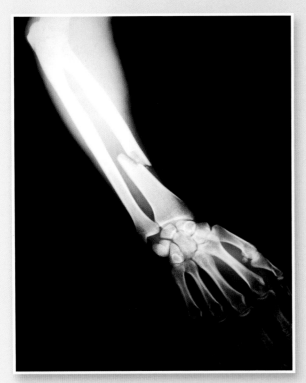

X-ray
An X-ray casts shadows on photographic film. Dense material, such as a bone, stops the rays and shows up on the film making breaks easy to see.

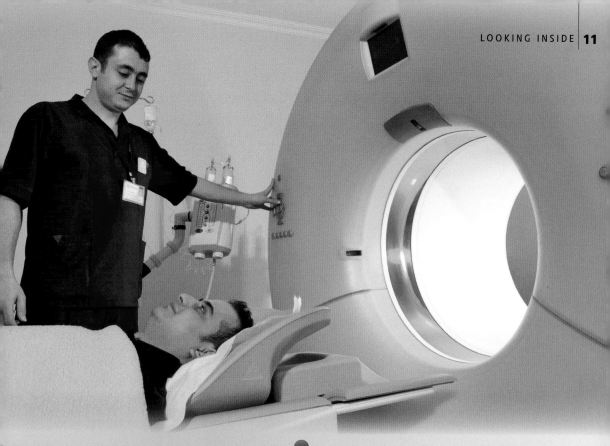

MRI scanner
The patient slides into the bore, or tube, through the center of a large magnet. Radio waves then map the body and provide a 3-D image of inside the body.

The magnetic field of an MRI scanner is up to 40,000 times greater than Earth's.

Ultrasound
The high-frequency sound waves that are used in an ultrasound are harmless to unborn babies. For pregnant mothers, an ultrasound image is often their baby's first "photograph."

Treatment

One of the best ways to treat patients is by giving them liquid drugs or nutrients, a little at a time, over a long period of time. The infusion pump does this job much more efficiently than a nurse or doctor. The pump can deliver as little as 0.003 fluid ounces (0.1 ml) of fluids an hour. A needle is inserted, usually into a vein in the back of the hand or the arm. Because the needles go into veins they are called intravenous, or IV, infusions. Tubes from the infusion pump deliver the fluids, very slowly, straight into the patient's bloodstream.

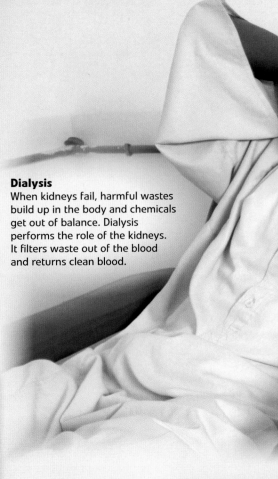

Dialysis
When kidneys fail, harmful wastes build up in the body and chemicals get out of balance. Dialysis performs the role of the kidneys. It filters waste out of the blood and returns clean blood.

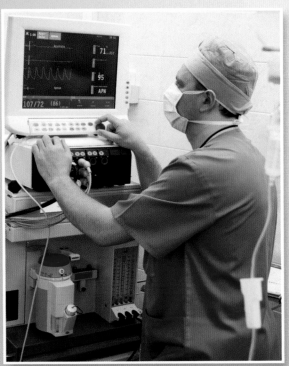

Blood transfusion
People often donate blood for use in blood transfusions. The word comes from the Latin *trans*, meaning "across."

Anesthesia
An anesthetist uses an IV infusion to anesthetize a patient. He then watches vital signs on a monitor.

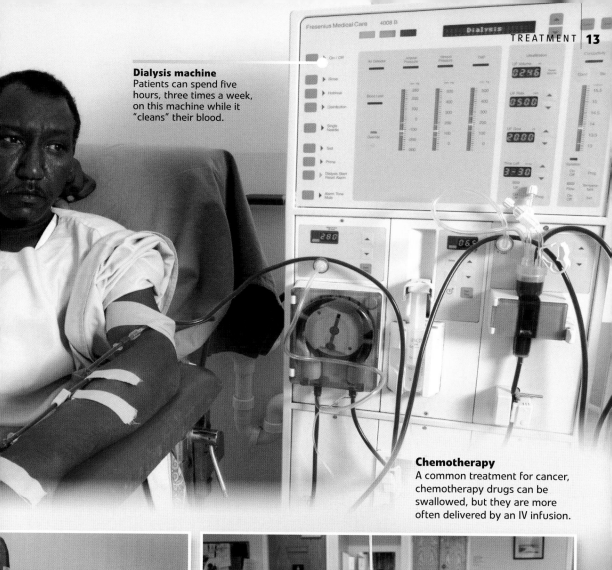

Fresenius Medical Care   4008 B

Dialysis

Dialysis machine
Patients can spend five
hours, three times a week,
on this machine while it
"cleans" their blood.

Chemotherapy
A common treatment for cancer,
chemotherapy drugs can be
swallowed, but they are more
often delivered by an IV infusion.

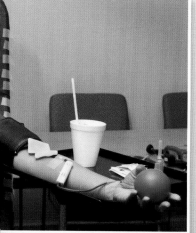

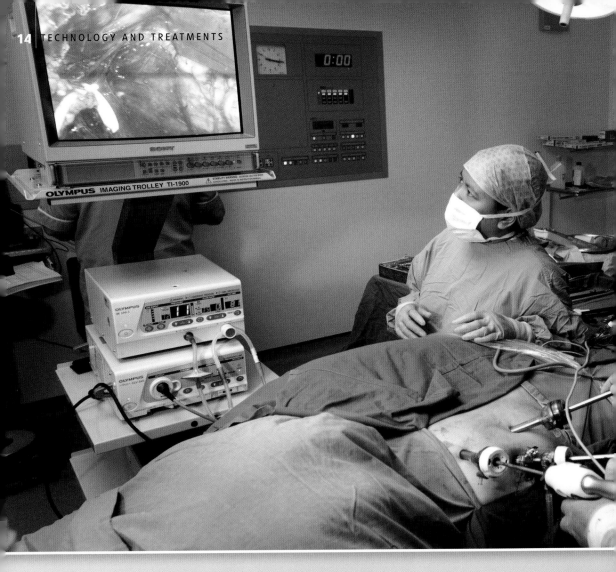

Operating Room

I n the past, operating room surgeons made large cuts, or incisions, in the patient's body. This was the only way they could see what they were doing, and get their hands inside to operate. But patients could die from blood loss, heart failure, or bacterial infections. They also needed many stitches to close the incision and took a long time to recover. Modern technologies, such as tiny cameras, special scalpels, and robots, now allow some operations to be done with smaller incisions, and operations are less risky for patients.

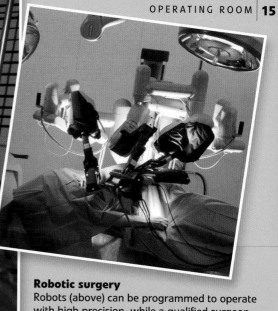

Robotic surgery
Robots (above) can be programmed to operate with high precision, while a qualified surgeon controls what the robot is doing.

Keyhole surgery
Keyhole, or laparoscopic, surgery requires only tiny incisions. The laparoscope (black handle) has a video camera, which is moved around inside the body so the surgeon can see what he is doing with his operating tools (silver handles).

Laser scalpel
Laser beams burn rather than cut. The heat seals blood vessels, so the patient loses less blood.

Endoscope
This thin tube has a tiny video camera at its tip and can be inserted in any opening of the body.

Replacement Parts

B ody parts can be affected by disease, damaged in accidents, or simply suffer wear and tear over time. If they cannot be saved, they might have to be replaced. Replacement parts can be living human organs, such as skin grafts or transplants of a heart or kidney. Other replacement parts, called prostheses, are manmade. False teeth, glass eyes, and wooden legs were among the first prostheses. Today, new replacement parts are made of lightweight materials, such as titanium and graphite, which can be shaped with great accuracy. Computer sensors or small batteries allow them to work almost as well as the parts they replace.

Myoelectric hand
Electrodes on the skin pick up signals from muscles to switch motors that operate this artificial hand. The hand can grip even small objects.

Knee replacement
A knee, worn out or crippled by arthritis, can be replaced by a titanium knee. The hinged joint mimics a normal knee joint.

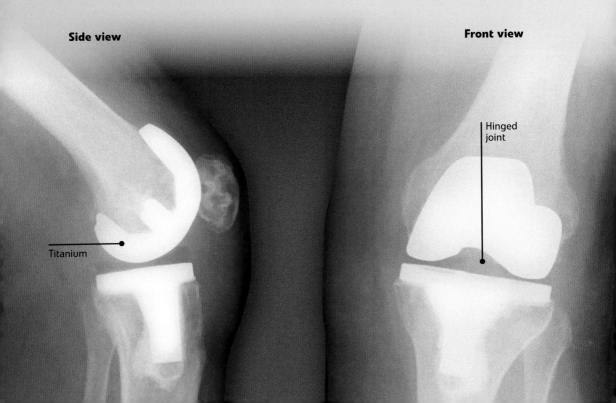

Side view

Front view

Titanium

Hinged joint

Bionic man

Doctors can now replace all four limbs and the joints where bones meet. They can also replace the heart, lungs, kidneys, and small sections of the brain.

Pacemaker

Shoulder replacement

Brain implant

Cochlear implant

Artificial lung

Artificial arm

Artificial heart

Elbow replacement

Artificial vertebrae

Spring-loaded leg

Artificial legs, especially for athletes, use strong but light springs. These allow the athlete to push off using less energy.

Hip replacement

Artificial hand

Knee replacement

Artificial leg

Eyes and Ears

S ight and hearing are important senses. For nearsighted or farsighted people who must wear glasses or contact lenses, laser eye surgery can correct these problems. Implanted lenses and transplanted corneas help people with more severe eye damage. Hearing-aid technology helps those whose hearing is damaged. But, for the totally or profoundly deaf, an external hearing aid does not work, and they need a "bionic ear," or cochlear implant. This sends signals to the auditory nerve in the brain and allows the deaf to hear.

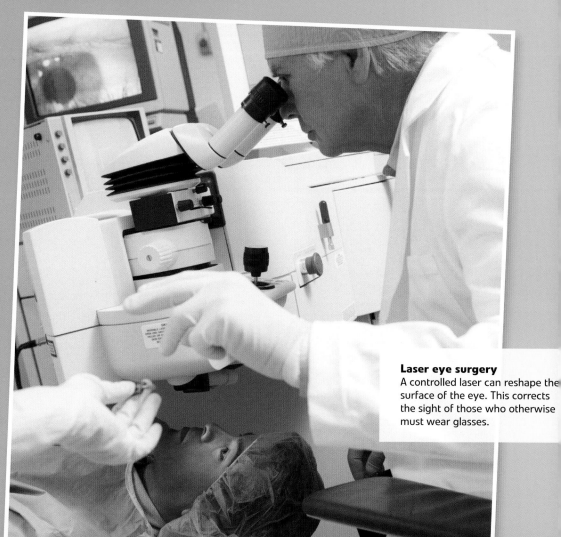

Laser eye surgery
A controlled laser can reshape the surface of the eye. This corrects the sight of those who otherwise must wear glasses.

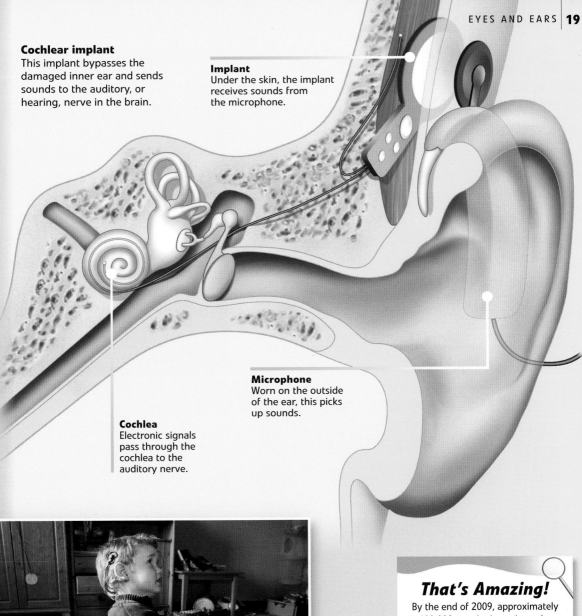

Cochlear implant
This implant bypasses the damaged inner ear and sends sounds to the auditory, or hearing, nerve in the brain.

Implant
Under the skin, the implant receives sounds from the microphone.

Cochlea
Electronic signals pass through the cochlea to the auditory nerve.

Microphone
Worn on the outside of the ear, this picks up sounds.

That's Amazing!
By the end of 2009, approximately 188,000 people throughout the world had undergone surgery to fit a cochlear implant.

A world of sound
A child as young as two years old can now be fitted with a cochlear implant.

Brain and Skull

The brain is the master organ that controls the body—all body movements, the five senses, thought, language, memory, and feelings. A brain surgeon must know exactly which part of a patient's brain is used for each of these functions before operating, to avoid causing blindness or paralysis during surgery. The most important technologies are therefore the ones that map the brain with pinpoint accuracy. The hard skull, and spaces in the brain filled with fluid, protect the brain. Problems arise when this fluid builds up.

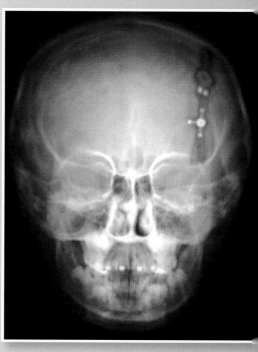

Smart shunt
Chambers inside the brain, called ventricles, contain fluid. When a ventricle has too much fluid, a shunt (red) is placed in the brain to drain it. This relieves pressure on the brain.

Cranial helmet
Some infants have flat-head syndrome, when pressure on the soft skull flattens part of it. Specially made cranial helmets reshape the infant's head over time.

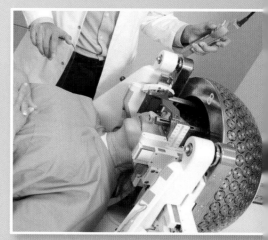

Gamma knife
This knife has no blade, does not cut, and draws no blood. It is a technology that delivers gamma radiation directly to a small brain tumor.

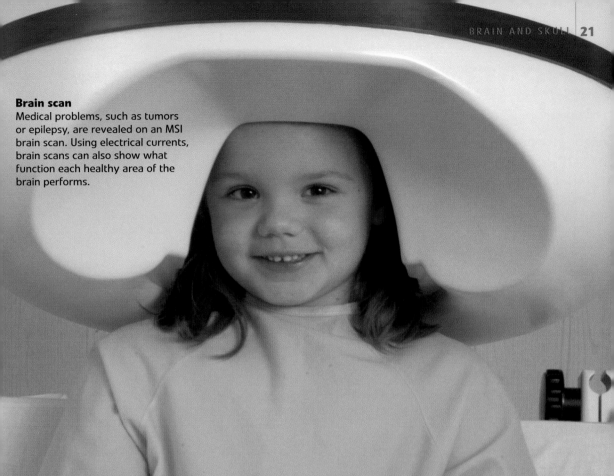

Brain scan
Medical problems, such as tumors or epilepsy, are revealed on an MSI brain scan. Using electrical currents, brain scans can also show what function each healthy area of the brain performs.

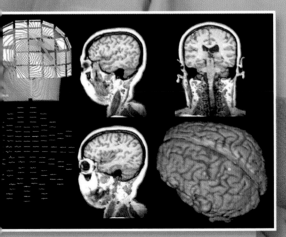

Magnetic Source Imaging (MSI)
MSI is a technology that combines different brain scans. It gives surgeons an accurate 3-D model of a patient's brain and brain functions.

Heart

The heart muscle is a muscle that pumps blood. Arteries carry blood away from the heart, and veins carry blood back to it. Heart valves make sure blood flows in the right direction. The heart's natural pacemaker keeps the heart rhythm steady. Any one of these parts can become damaged or fail. If the heart fails, the body dies. Heart surgeons use a wide range of technologies to keep hearts operating, including a defibrillator to restart a heart that has stopped beating.

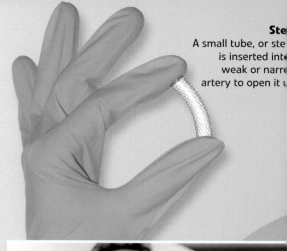

Ste
A small tube, or ste
is inserted int
weak or narr
artery to open it u

Valves
If one of the heart's four valves fails, an artificial valve can be implanted. This keeps blood flowing in the right direction.

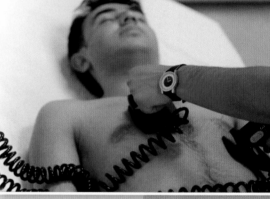

Defibrillator
A defibrillator gives the heart an electric shock to restore the normal heart rhythm.

Manmade pacemaker
A manmade pacemaker can keep the heart beating at the correct rate of 70–80 beats a minute.

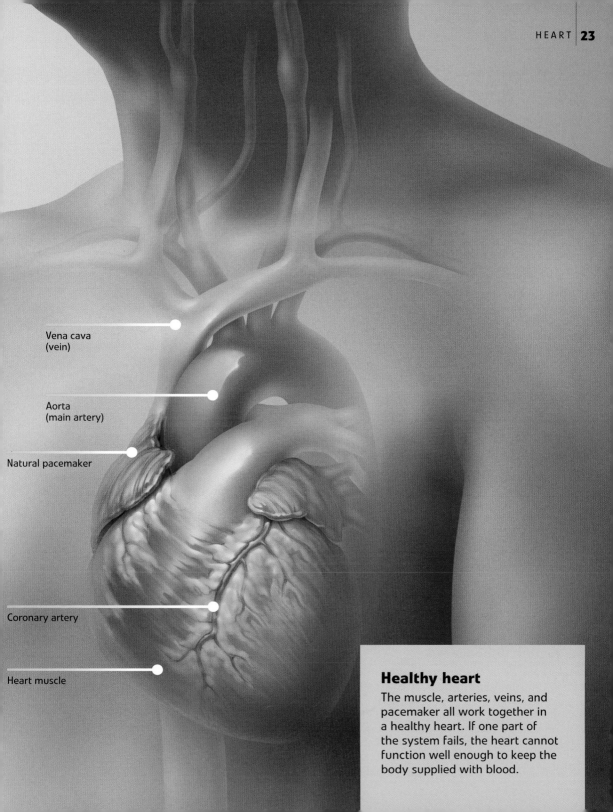

Vena cava
(vein)

Aorta
(main artery)

Natural pacemaker

Coronary artery

Heart muscle

Healthy heart

The muscle, arteries, veins, and pacemaker all work together in a healthy heart. If one part of the system fails, the heart cannot function well enough to keep the body supplied with blood.

Transplants

Doctors can transplant most of the body's main organs, except for the brain. The three sources of new organs are: a healthy organ from someone who has died; an organ, such as a kidney, from a live donor; or a manmade organ, such as an artificial heart. Central databases match the blood and tissue of the patient and the person who gives the organ, called the donor. Even with a good match, the body's immune system does not recognize the "foreign" cells in the new organ, and tries to reject it. Transplant patients must take antirejection medication.

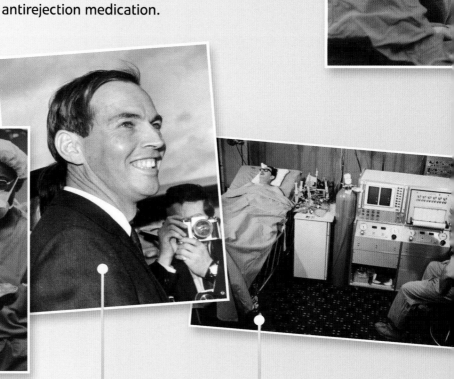

1967
Dr. Thomas Startzl
successfully transplanted
a liver into a patient
at a hospital in
Denver, Colorado.

1967
South African surgeon
Dr. Christiaan Barnard
became famous when
he performed the first
successful heart transplant.

1968
Patient Haskell Karp
rests following his
surgery for an artificial
heart implant at the
Texas Heart Institute.

1979
In Minnesota, part of a
mother's pancreas was
successfully transplante
her child—the first panc
transplant with a live do

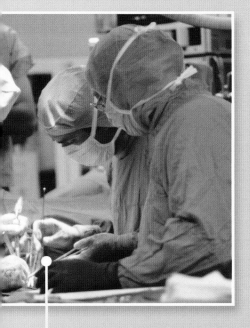

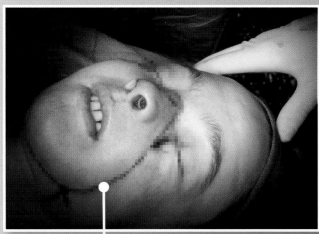

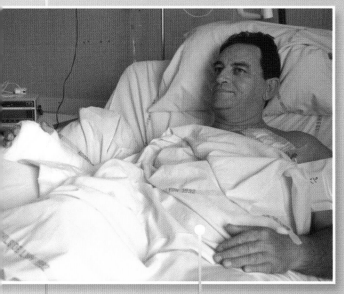

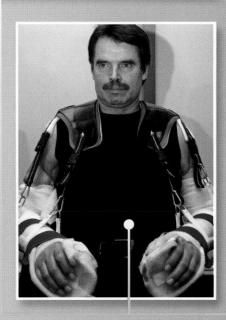

ruce Reitz and his
transplanted a
and two lungs into
ear-old Mary Gohlke
Arizona.

1998
Patient Clint Hallam
recovers in a hospital in
France after a 13-hour
operation that grafted
on a new right hand.

2005
Isabelle Dinoir, whose face
was badly bitten by a dog,
received a partial face
transplant (nose, lips, and
chin) in a French hospital.

2008
Karl Merk, a German
farmer who lost his
arms in 2002, became
the first patient to receive
two transplanted arms.

?... **You Decide**

The stem cells in a fertilized human egg are all the same. As the embryo grows, the stem cells grow into the different types of body cells, such as nerve, muscle, bone, and skin cells. Scientists can grow body cells from stem cells in a laboratory. But should they?

For stem cell research

Scientists can grow new cells and tissues to treat many diseases. In the future, they might even be able to grow new organs.

Your own stem cells
A baby's umbilical cord is rich in stem cells. These could be kept to repair damaged cells later in life.

Stem cell treatment
Spinal cord injuries, such as those suffered by *Superman* actor Christopher Reeve, could be treated with stem cells.

Cloning
Every human being's DNA is unique. Stem cells could be used to clone, or grow, identical human beings.

Stem cell source
Where do stem cells come from—embryo or adult? Was an embryo used and a possible human life destroyed?

gainst stem ell research
ost stem cell research uses nbryonic stem cells, but an nbryo, or fertilized egg, is a ture human being, not just collection of cells in a lab dish.

Developments

New technologies take many years to develop, test, and then try out on human patients. But medical researchers can borrow technology. New handheld scanners send medical test results using cell phone technology. The US space program has developed technologies that will soon be available to others. There is no doctor on board a spacecraft, so astronauts need technology they can operate themselves—and it needs to be small. NASA scientists are working on small, portable X-ray machines and nanotechnology. Nano drugs will be built on the atomic scale.

Space technology
The US space program is constantly developing new technologies. Some of these will soon be available to patients on Earth.

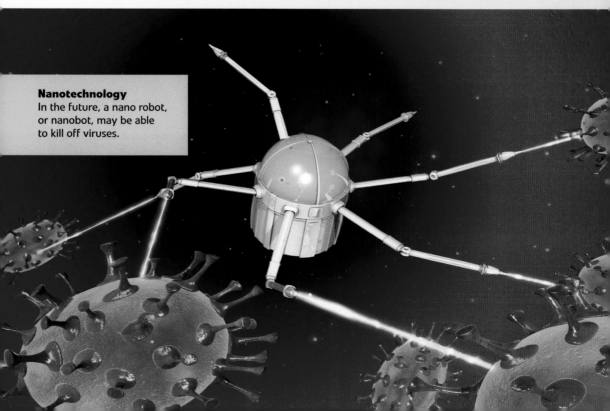

Nanotechnology
In the future, a nano robot, or nanobot, may be able to kill off viruses.

Handheld EKG

This mobile electrocardiograph (ECG or EKG) measures heart functions. It displays and memorizes cardiograms. These can then be sent to a doctor by cell phone.

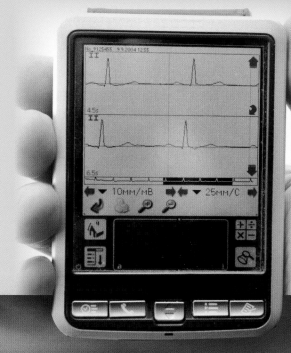

ndheld X–ray

e latest X-ray machines can be held in one nd. Dentists and security guards may find em useful, but radiation dose is a concern.

Retina implant

A tiny chip might one day replace damaged light-detecting cells in the retina of the eye. The chip would change light into nerve signals sent to the brain.

Fact File

Medical treatments and technologies have a long history and change dramatically over time. New breakthroughs, which seem wonderful when they are first invented, often seem very clumsy and old-fashioned in later years.

Here are some strange and unusual facts about medical breakthroughs:

1 Victims of polio, whose chest muscles were paralyzed, spent long periods (in one case 60 years) in iron lungs, which breathed for them. Modern ventilators do the same job but are not as terrifying as the iron lung must have been for children with polio.

2 If he had been born today, US president George Washington could have teeth implants made of titanium and porcelain. Instead, his false teeth, or dentures, had a plate made of hippopotamus ivory, with ivory, human, or horses' teeth.

3 Wooden, or peg, legs were the only form of artificial leg available until the nineteenth century. US senator Gouverneur Morris could do no more than "stump" on his leg, unlike Olympic athletes today who run on lightweight metal legs with springs.

4 The first contact lenses were made from glass molds of rabbits' eyes. Glass lenses deprived the eye of oxygen, caused infections, and could be worn for only an hour or two. The plastics used in contact lenses today have none of these problems.

1 Iron lung, 1938

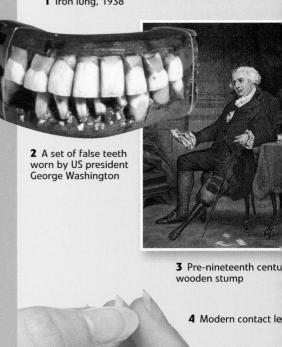

2 A set of false teeth worn by US president George Washington

3 Pre-nineteenth centu[ry] wooden stump

4 Modern contact le[nses]

Glossary

clone (KLOHN) To create an identical human being or animal.

cochlear implant (KO-klee-ur IM-plant) An electronic device that stimulates nerves in the cochlea.

cranial helmet (KRAY-nee-ul HEL-mit) A medical helmet that corrects the shape of an infant's skull.

defibrillator (dee-FIH-brih-lay-tur) A device that delivers electric shocks to restart or restore the rhythm of the heart.

donor (DOH-nur) A person, alive or dead, who gives, or donates, an organ for transplant into another person.

eliminate (ih-LIH-muh-nayt) To cut out or get rid of.

embryo (EM-bree-oh) An animal in its earliest stage of development—up to eight weeks for a human baby.

endoscope (EN-doh-skohp) An instrument, with a camera attached, that doctors insert into the body to examine organs.

gamma knife (GA-muh NYF) An instrument that emits beams of gamma radiation directly at a tumor without cutting the skin.

infusion pump (in-FYOO-zhun PUMP) A device that delivers a small, measured amount of fluid into the bloodstream over a period of time.

intravenous (IV) (in-truh-VEE-nus) Describes the delivery of fluid into a vein.

laparoscopic surgery (la-pruh-SKAH-pik SER-juh-ree) Surgery that requires only a small incision, or cut.

magnetic resonance imaging (MRI) (mag-NEH-tik REH-za-nints IH-mij-ing) A medical technique that uses magnetism, radio waves, and a computer to take pictures inside the body.

nanotechnology (na-noh-tek-NAH-luh-jee) The science of making things, such as robots, on a tiny scale. Nano means one billionth.

pacemaker (PAYS-may-ker) A natural system in the heart, or a manmade electronic device, that sends electrical impulses to the heart muscle to keep it beating in a normal rhythm.

paramedic (pa-reh-MEH-dik) A health care professional who assists a doctor. Ambulance workers, medical technicians, and nurses are all paramedics.

prostheses (prahs-THEE-seez) Artificial, or manmade, replacements of a part of the body such as a leg, arm, hip, eye, or knee.

shunt (SHUNT) A manmade, narrow tube that diverts excess fluid in one part of the body to a different area.

spirometer (spy-RAH-mih-ter) An instrument that measures the amount of air entering and leaving the lungs.

stem cell (STEM SEL) An unspecialized cell that can grow into any other type of body cell, such as a blood cell, skin cell, muscle cell, nerve cell, or bone cell.

stent (STENT) An artificial tube inserted into a vessel or passageway, such as an artery, to keep it open.

ultrasound (UL-truh-sownd) A method of creating an image of an organ inside the body by using high-frequency sound waves.

Index

Websites

Due to the changing nature of Internet links, PowerKids Press has developed an online list of websites related to the subject of this book. This site is updated regularly. Please use this link to access the list: www.powerkidslinks.com/disc/tech/